Scott Foresman

Math Around the Clock

SUMMER SCHOOL • AFTER SCHOOL • INTERSESSION

Understanding Fractions

PEARSON

Scott Foresman

Editorial Offices:
Glenview, Illinois • Parsippany, New Jersey • New York, New York

Sales Offices:
Parsippany, New Jersey • Duluth, Georgia • Glenview, Illinois
Coppell, Texas • Ontario, California • Mesa, Arizona

ISBN: 0-328-06369-X

2 3 4 5 6 7 8 9 10 V004 12 11 10 09 08 07 06 05 04 03

Math Around the Clock

Contents

Unit 4 • Understanding Fractions

Think about the prime numbers from 2 to 100. The greatest number of primes have what digit in the ones place?

Prime Factorization

Example

Use a factor tree to find the prime factorization of 240. Then write the product using exponents.

Write 240 as a product of two factors. This can be done in more than one way. Write each factor that is not prime as a product.

When all the branches end in prime numbers, you can write the prime factorization. The primes are usually written from least to greatest. Whenever factors appear more than once, exponents can be used.

$$240 = 2^4 \times 3 \times 5$$

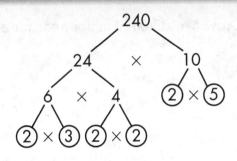

Complete each factor tree. Write the prime factorization with exponents, if you can.

1 21
___ × ___

___

2 24

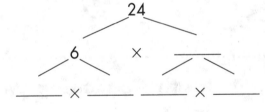

3 81

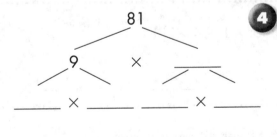

4 56

Prime Factorization (continued)

Draw two different factor trees for each number.

5 45   **6** 36   **7** 42

If the number is prime, write *prime*. If the number is composite, write the prime factorization of the number.

8 11   **9** 18   **10** 41   **11** 40

_____   _____   _____   _____

12 16   **13** 17   **14** 80   **15** 95

_____   _____   _____   _____

16 35   **17** 72   **18** 48   **19** 55

_____   _____   _____   _____

20 **Math Reasoning** What number has a prime factorization of $2^3 \times 7$?

_____

21 Holly says the prime factorization for 44 is 4×11.
Is she right? Why or why not?

_____

22 **Test Prep** Choose the correct letter for each answer.

Find the prime factorization for 12.

A 4×3 **B** 2×3 **C** $2^2 \times 3$ **D** 2×3^2

23 Find the prime number.

F 55   **G** 15   **H** 41   **J** 39

Prime Factorization

1 Which statement is true about a prime number?

A It has exactly three factors.

B It must be an odd number.

C It must be greater than 10.

D It has exactly two factors, itself and 1.

2 Which is the prime factorization of 48?

F $2^3 \times 3$ **H** 3×16

G $2^4 \times 3$ **J** 6×8

3 Which number is composite?

A 24   **C** 53

B 31   **D** 97

4 Which is the prime factorization of 180?

F $2 \times 3^2 \times 10$

G 5×3^4

H $2^2 \times 3^2 \times 5$

J $2 \times 5 \times 18$

5 Which is *not* a prime number?

A 51   **C** 43

B 47   **D** 41

6 Which is a prime number?

F 1   **H** 27

G 17   **J** 39

7 What is the prime factorization of 495?

A $5 \times 11 \times 3^2$

B $5 \times 11 \times 3$

C 5×11^2

D $5 \times 11 \times 9$

8 Which number is not composite?

F 35   **H** 57

G 49   **J** 61

9 Which expression shows 100 as a product of prime factors?

A 4×25 **C** $2^2 \times 5^2$

B 10×10 **D** $2^3 \times 5^2$

10 Ciandra lives on a block with house numbers from 31 to 61. If everyone on the block has a prime house number, how many houses are there on the block?

F 2 houses   **H** 8 houses

G 6 houses   **J** 15 houses

Oral Directions Choose the correct letter for each answer.

Find two fractions that are greater than $\frac{1}{2}$ but less than 1. How many others can you name? Show your answers on a number line.

Name _____

Example

What fraction should be written at Point *A*?

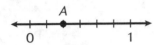

There are 6 equal parts between 0 and 1. Point *A* shows 2 of the 6 equal parts. So, $\frac{2}{6}$ should be written at Point *A*.

....

What fraction should be written at each point?

1 Point *A* _____

2 Point *B* _____

3 Point *C* _____

4 Point *L* _____

5 Point *M* _____

6 Point *N* _____

7 Point *R* _____

8 Point *S* _____

9 Point *T* _____

Name _____

Fractions on a Number Line (continued)

What fraction should be written at each point?

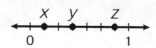

10 Point X _____   **11** Point Y _____   **12** Point Z _____

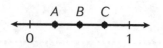

13 Point A _____   **14** Point B _____   **15** Point C _____

16 Draw 0 and 1 on a number line. Then show $\frac{3}{7}$ and $\frac{6}{7}$.

17 **Math Reasoning** What number is halfway between $\frac{2}{4}$ and $\frac{3}{4}$ on a number line? _____

18 Write the missing measures on the ruler shown.

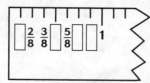

19 **Test Prep** Choose the correct letter for the answer.

Give the missing fraction:

A $\frac{2}{4}$ **B** $\frac{1}{4}$ **C** $\frac{2}{3}$ **D** $\frac{1}{3}$

Name _____

Fractions on a Number Line

1 Find the fraction shown by Point *P*.

A $\frac{1}{10}$ **C** $\frac{8}{10}$

B $\frac{7}{10}$ **D** $\frac{10}{10}$

2 Find the fraction shown by Point *V*.

F $\frac{1}{6}$ **H** $\frac{3}{6}$

G $\frac{2}{6}$ **J** $\frac{2}{4}$

3 Which letter is at $\frac{3}{7}$ on the number line?

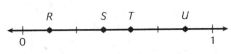

A *R*   **C** *T*

B *S*   **D** *U*

4 Which letter is at $\frac{1}{4}$ on the number line?

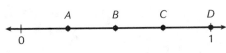

F *A*   **H** *C*

G *B*   **J** *D*

5 Find the fraction shown by Point *H*.

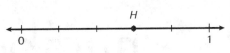

A $\frac{3}{10}$ **C** $\frac{3}{6}$

B $\frac{2}{5}$ **D** $\frac{3}{5}$

6 Which letter is at $\frac{4}{9}$ on the number line?

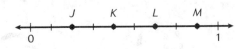

F *J*   **H** *L*

G *K*   **J** *M*

7 Find the fraction shown by Point *S*.

A $\frac{1}{8}$ **C** $\frac{7}{4}$

B $\frac{6}{8}$ **D** $1\frac{1}{8}$

8 Which letter is at $\frac{4}{6}$ on the number line?

F *W*   **H** *Y*

G *X*   **J** *Z*

Oral Directions Choose the correct letter for each answer.

Write three decimal numbers that are between $\frac{1}{5}$ and $\frac{1}{4}$.

(Hint: Change these fractions to decimals.)

Name _____

Example

Write a fraction and a decimal for the shaded parts of the set.

$\frac{2}{5}$ of the shapes are shaded.

$\frac{2}{5} = 2 \div 5 = 0.4$ $\qquad$ $5\overline{)2.0}^{\,0.4}$

Write a fraction and a decimal for each shaded part.

1

_____

2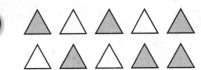

_____

3

_____

4

_____

5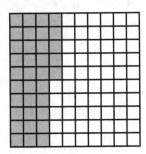

_____

6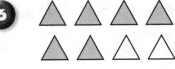

_____

Name _____

Relating Fractions and Decimals (continued)

Write a fraction and a decimal for each shaded part.

 7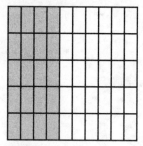

_____

8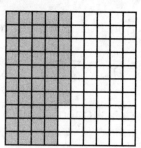

_____

9

_____

10 ○○○○○ ○○○○○

_____

Use the number line to write a fraction and a decimal for each point.

11 Point X

_____

12 Point Y

_____

13 Point Z

_____

14 **Math Reasoning** Write $\frac{1}{4}$ as a decimal. What is $\frac{1}{4}$ of a dollar? How are these two numbers related?

_____

15 Mary has 6 stuffed animals. Three of them are bears and 2 of them are rabbits. Write a fraction and a decimal to represent the bears. _____

16 **Test Prep** Choose the correct letter for the answer.

Find the decimal that is the same as $\frac{12}{50}$.

A 0.12   **B** 0.06   **C** 0.24   **D** 0.50

Name _____

1 Which fraction and decimal describes the shaded part?

A $\frac{1}{4}$ and 0.25

B $\frac{1}{2}$ and 0.5

C $\frac{3}{4}$ and 0.75

D $\frac{3}{4}$ and 0.3

2 Which of the following is equal to $\frac{1}{4}$?

F 0.14   H 0.25

G 0.20   J 0.40

3 Shawn bought 0.5 pound of strawberries. Which fraction is equal to 0.5?

A $\frac{1}{50}$ C $\frac{5}{10}$

B $\frac{1}{5}$ D $\frac{50}{10}$

4 Which of the following is equal to 0.2?

F $\frac{2}{100}$ H $\frac{1}{2}$

G $\frac{1}{5}$ J $\frac{2}{1}$

5 Which is a fraction and a decimal for 3 tenths?

A $\frac{3}{100}$ and 0.03

B $\frac{3}{10}$ and 0.3

C $\frac{1}{3}$ and 0.3

D $\frac{3}{3}$ and 1

6 Which is a fraction and a decimal for Point P?

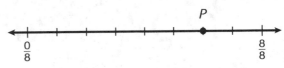

F $\frac{3}{8}$ and 0.375 H $\frac{5}{8}$ and 0.75

G $\frac{4}{8}$ and 0.5   J $\frac{6}{8}$ and 0.75

7 Which is a decimal for 8 hundredths?

A 0.08   C 8.0

B 0.8   D 800

8 Which decimal describes the number of faces that are not smiling?

F 0.2   H 0.6

G 0.25   J 0.75

Oral Directions Choose the correct letter for each answer.

Michael bought
5 pounds of peanuts.
He put equal amounts
in each of 2 bags.
How many pounds
were in each bag?

Fractions and Division

Example

Find $12 \div 5$.

Give the answer as a fraction, a mixed number, or a whole number.

$12 \div 5 = \dfrac{12}{5}$, or $2\dfrac{2}{5}$

Give each answer as a fraction, a mixed number, or a whole number.

1 $\quad 2 \div 6 =$ _____

2 $\quad 3 \div 2 =$ _____

3 $\quad 7 \div 9 =$ _____

4 $\quad 1 \div 5 =$ _____

5 $\quad 13 \div 2 =$ _____

6 $\quad 3 \div 4 =$ _____

7 $\quad 2 \div 8 =$ _____

8 $\quad 15 \div 3 =$ _____

9 $\quad 8 \div 9 =$ _____

10 $\quad 10 \div 4 =$ _____

11 $\quad 12 \div 3 =$ _____

12 $\quad 6 \div 8 =$ _____

13 $\quad 7 \div 10 =$ _____

14 $\quad 12 \div 11 =$ _____

15 $\quad 18 \div 6 =$ _____

16 $\quad 2 \div 5 =$ _____

17 $\quad 5 \div 2 =$ _____

18 $\quad 9 \div 13 =$ _____

Fractions and Division (continued)

Give each answer as a fraction, a mixed number, or a whole number.

19 $6 \div 2 =$ _____   **20** $7 \div 2 =$ _____   **21** $3 \div 9 =$ _____

22 $1 \div 4 =$ _____   **23** $15 \div 2 =$ _____   **24** $3 \div 5 =$ _____

25 **Algebra** Evaluate $x \div 3$ for $x = 7$.   _____

26 Carlton has 3 apples to share between 4 friends. How much of an apple will each friend receive?   _____

27 Mrs. Savage baked 5 apple pies and used 4 apples to make each pie. She is dividing the pies among 3 different dishes to give to friends. How much pie will be in each dish?   _____

28 Eddie and 2 friends are cleaning the chalkboard for their teacher. Four other students are cleaning 5 erasers. How much of the chalkboard will each student clean?   _____

29 **Test Prep** Choose the correct letter for each answer.

Find $16 \div 3$.

A $\frac{3}{16}$ **B** $5\frac{3}{1}$ **C** $5\frac{1}{3}$ **D** $4\frac{4}{3}$

30 Fred and Max are mowing 3 acres of land. How many acres will each boy mow?

F $1\frac{1}{2}$ **G** $\frac{2}{3}$ **H** $\frac{5}{3}$ **J** $\frac{3}{5}$

Name _____

Fractions and Division

1 Mrs. Lopez has 1 apple. She wants her 4 children to share the apple equally. How much will each child get?

    A $\frac{1}{4}$ apple   **D** 4 apples

    B $\frac{1}{2}$ apple   **E** NH

    C $\frac{3}{4}$ apple

2 Find $3 \div 10$.

    F $\frac{3}{10}$ **J** $3\frac{1}{3}$

    G $\frac{1}{3}$ **K** NH

    H $3\frac{1}{10}$

3 Bagels are sold in packages of 6. Mr. Henderson has 18 bagels. How many packages did Mr. Henderson buy?

    A $\frac{1}{6}$ package

    B $\frac{6}{18}$ package

    C 2 packages

    D 4 packages

    E NH

4 Find $7 \div 2$.

    F $\frac{2}{7}$ **J** $3\frac{1}{2}$

    G $2\frac{1}{2}$ **K** NH

    H 3

5 Find $5 \div 7$.

    A $1\frac{2}{5}$ **D** $\frac{5}{7}$

    B $1\frac{2}{7}$ **E** NH

    C $\frac{7}{5}$

6 Ryan bought a pound of cheese. He sliced the cheese into 8 equal pieces. How much does each slice weigh?

    F $\frac{1}{10}$ pound   **J** 1 pound

    G $\frac{1}{8}$ pound   **K** NH

    H $\frac{1}{2}$ pound

7 Find $4 \div 3$.

    A $\frac{3}{4}$ **D** $1\frac{1}{3}$

    B $1\frac{1}{12}$ **E** NH

    C $1\frac{1}{4}$

Oral Directions Choose the correct letter for each answer.

Use the following four digits to write 2 equivalent fractions: 3, 6, 2, 1.

Equivalent Fractions

Example 1

Use multiplication to find a fraction that is equivalent to $\frac{3}{7}$.

Multiply the numerator and
denominator by the same number.

$3 \longrightarrow \times 2 = \frac{6}{14}$
$7 \longrightarrow \times 2 = $

Example 2

Use division to write a fraction that is equivalent to $\frac{16}{20}$.

Think of a number that is a factor of both 16 and 20.

2 is a factor of both 16 and 20.
Divide the numerator and denominator by that factor.

$$\frac{16 \div 2}{20 \div 2} = \frac{8}{10}$$

If you continue to divide until 1 is the only factor
of both the numerator and the denominator, you
find the fraction in simplest form.

$$\frac{16 \div 2}{20 \div 2} = \frac{8}{10} \div 2 = \frac{4}{5}$$

$\frac{8}{10}$ and $\frac{4}{5}$ are both equivalent to $\frac{16}{20}$. Only $\frac{4}{5}$ is in simplest form.

1 $\quad \frac{1}{4} = \frac{}{8}$

2 $\quad \frac{5}{10} = \frac{}{2}$

3 $\quad \frac{2}{3} = \frac{}{9}$

4 $\quad \frac{7}{9} = \frac{}{36}$

5 $\quad \frac{6}{15} = \frac{}{5}$

6 $\quad \frac{18}{24} = \frac{}{4}$

7 $\quad \frac{5}{3} = \frac{}{12}$

8 $\quad \frac{12}{20} = \frac{}{5}$

9 $\quad \frac{4}{7} = \frac{}{21}$

Name _____

Equivalent Fractions (continued)

10 $\frac{1}{5} = \frac{}{15}$ **11** $\frac{8}{10} = \frac{}{5}$ **12** $\frac{2}{8} = \frac{}{4}$

13 $\frac{7}{10} = \frac{}{20}$ **14** $\frac{6}{14} = \frac{}{7}$ **15** $\frac{8}{11} = \frac{}{22}$

Write a fraction or mixed number equivalent to the fraction shown.

16 $\frac{3}{7}$ _____   **17** $\frac{1}{8}$ _____   **18** $2\frac{3}{5}$ _____   **19** $\frac{6}{10}$ _____

Write each fraction or mixed number in simplest form.

20 $\frac{9}{12}$ _____   **21** $\frac{10}{15}$ _____   **22** $1\frac{6}{8}$ _____   **23** $\frac{16}{24}$ _____

24 **Math Reasoning** Use 2 number lines to show that $\frac{1}{3}$ is the same as $\frac{2}{6}$.

25 On Tuesday, $\frac{2}{3}$ of the class time was spent on English projects. Write three equivalent fractions for $\frac{2}{3}$. _____

26 **Test Prep** Choose the correct letter for each answer.

Which fraction is equivalent to $\frac{5}{9}$?

A $\frac{10}{9}$ **B** $\frac{10}{18}$ **C** $\frac{15}{18}$ **D** $\frac{5}{18}$

27 Which fraction is in simplest form?

F $\frac{5}{6}$ **G** $\frac{4}{6}$ **H** $\frac{3}{6}$ **J** $\frac{2}{6}$

Name _____

1 Which fraction is equivalent to $\frac{5}{8}$?

A $\frac{4}{7}$ C $\frac{10}{16}$

B $\frac{5}{9}$ D $\frac{15}{20}$

2 Which of the following are equivalent fractions for $\frac{6}{18}$?

F $\frac{1}{3}$ and $\frac{3}{9}$

G $\frac{1}{3}$ and $\frac{2}{9}$

H $\frac{1}{4}$ and $\frac{3}{9}$

J $\frac{1}{4}$ and $\frac{2}{8}$

3 Which number belongs in the ■?

$$2\frac{8}{10} = 2\frac{■}{5}$$

A 3   C 8

B 4   D 16

4 Which fraction is equivalent to $\frac{2}{3}$?

F $\frac{2}{6}$ H $\frac{12}{18}$

G $\frac{2}{4}$ J $\frac{16}{20}$

5 Which fraction is equivalent to $\frac{3}{5}$?

A $\frac{1}{3}$ C $\frac{6}{10}$

B $\frac{2}{7}$ D $\frac{9}{12}$

6 At the horse show, 6 of the 10 horses are brown. Which fraction, in simplest form, describes the horses that are brown?

F $\frac{4}{5}$ H $\frac{1}{2}$

G $\frac{3}{5}$ J $\frac{3}{10}$

7 Which shows a fraction that names the shaded part of the circle and another fraction that is equivalent to it?

A $\frac{4}{8}, \frac{1}{2}$ C $\frac{5}{8}, \frac{10}{16}$

B $\frac{4}{8}, \frac{2}{5}$ D $\frac{4}{8}, \frac{2}{6}$

Oral Directions Choose the correct letter for each answer.

© Scott Foresman

Tomas bought $\frac{3}{4}$ pound of red grapes and $\frac{10}{16}$ pound of green grapes. Did he buy more green grapes or red grapes? Explain your answer.

Name _____

Example

Find a fraction equivalent to $\frac{1}{6}$ with a denominator of 30.

$\frac{1}{6} = \frac{?}{30}$ $\frac{1}{6} = \frac{1 \times 5}{6 \times 5} = \frac{5}{30}$

So, $\frac{1}{6} = \frac{5}{30}$.

Find each equivalent fraction.

1 $\frac{2}{3} = \frac{}{18}$ **2** $\frac{3}{4} = \frac{}{20}$ **3** $\frac{5}{8} = \frac{}{56}$

4 $\frac{1}{4} = \frac{5}{}$ **5** $\frac{10}{35} = \frac{}{7}$ **6** $\frac{30}{48} = \frac{}{8}$

7 $\frac{5}{9} = \frac{25}{}$ **8** $\frac{14}{49} = \frac{2}{}$ **9** $\frac{12}{13} = \frac{}{26}$

10 $\frac{9}{27} = \frac{3}{}$ **11** $\frac{12}{48} = \frac{1}{}$ **12** $\frac{6}{7} = \frac{48}{}$

13 $\frac{7}{13} = \frac{}{39}$ **14** $\frac{2}{24} = \frac{}{12}$ **15** $\frac{54}{81} = \frac{6}{}$

Equivalent Fractions (continued)

Find each equivalent fraction.

16 $\dfrac{2}{3} = \dfrac{}{15}$

17 $\dfrac{3}{4} = \dfrac{}{24}$

18 $\dfrac{5}{8} = \dfrac{}{64}$

19 $\dfrac{1}{4} = \dfrac{7}{}$

20 $\dfrac{12}{42} = \dfrac{}{7}$

21 $\dfrac{35}{40} = \dfrac{}{8}$

22 $\dfrac{5}{9} = \dfrac{45}{}$

23 $\dfrac{16}{48} = \dfrac{2}{}$

24 $\dfrac{11}{13} = \dfrac{}{26}$

25 **Math Reasoning** Use a number line to show that $\dfrac{1}{3}$ is equal to $\dfrac{2}{6}$.

26 On Saturday, Yolanda spent $\dfrac{2}{3}$ of her day playing. How many ninths of her day was spent playing?

_____

27 Tom needs $\dfrac{3}{6}$ cup of paint for his model airplane. The store sells paint in $\dfrac{1}{2}$ cup containers. Will one container provide enough paint?

_____

28 **Test Prep** Choose the correct letter for the answer.

Which fraction is equivalent to $\dfrac{1}{5}$?

A $\dfrac{5}{20}$ **B** $\dfrac{5}{25}$ **C** $\dfrac{5}{10}$ **D** $\dfrac{5}{30}$

Name _____

1 Which number belongs in the ▪?

$$\frac{5}{7} = \frac{▪}{14}$$

A 6   **C** 10

B 7   **D** 12

5 Which fraction is equivalent to $\frac{5}{6}$ with a denominator of 36?

A $\frac{6}{36}$ **C** $\frac{35}{36}$

B $\frac{30}{36}$ **D** $\frac{36}{30}$

2 Which number belongs in the ▪?

$$\frac{18}{24} = \frac{3}{▪}$$

F 4   **H** 24

G 6   **J** 144

6 Which number belongs in the ▪?

$$\frac{48}{▪} = \frac{8}{15}$$

F 30   **H** 60

G 50   **J** 90

3 Continue the pattern. Which fractions come next?

$$\frac{32}{64}, \frac{16}{32}, \frac{8}{16}, \underline{\quad}, \underline{\quad}$$

A $\frac{4}{8}, \frac{2}{4}$ **C** $\frac{5}{8}, \frac{1}{4}$

B $\frac{6}{8}, \frac{3}{4}$ **D** $\frac{3}{8}, \frac{2}{4}$

7 Which number belongs in the ▪?

$$\frac{▪}{9} = \frac{20}{36}$$

A 15   **C** 6

B 10   **D** 5

4 Which number belongs in the ▪?

$$\frac{7}{▪} = \frac{28}{32}$$

F 6   **H** 14

G 8   **J** 16

8 Continue the pattern. Which fractions come next?

$$\frac{4}{5}, \frac{8}{10}, \frac{12}{15}, \frac{16}{20}, \underline{\quad}, \underline{\quad}$$

F $\frac{18}{21}, \frac{21}{24}$ **H** $\frac{20}{25}, \frac{24}{30}$

G $\frac{20}{15}, \frac{24}{15}$ **J** $\frac{25}{20}, \frac{30}{24}$

Oral Directions Choose the correct letter for each answer.

Write two fractions that are between 0 and $\frac{1}{2}$, and write two fractions that are between $\frac{1}{2}$ and 1.

Relating Fractions to One Half

Example

If a fraction is less than $\frac{1}{2}$, its numerator is less than half its denominator.

Is $\frac{3}{7}$ greater than or less than $\frac{1}{2}$?

$\frac{1}{2}$ of 7 is $7 \div 2 = 3.5$, $3 < 3.5$, so $\frac{3}{7} < \frac{1}{2}$

If a fraction is greater than $\frac{1}{2}$, its numerator is greater than

half its denominator. Is $\frac{11}{18}$ greater than or less than $\frac{1}{2}$?

$18 \div 2 = 9$, $11 > 9$ so $\frac{11}{18} > \frac{1}{2}$

Compare. Write >, <, or = for each ●.

1 $\quad \frac{1}{2} ● \frac{1}{6}$

2 $\quad \frac{1}{2} ● \frac{5}{7}$

3 $\quad \frac{3}{6} ● \frac{1}{2}$

4 $\quad \frac{4}{9} ● \frac{1}{2}$

5 $\quad \frac{7}{8} ● \frac{1}{2}$

6 $\quad \frac{5}{10} ● \frac{1}{2}$

7 $\quad \frac{1}{2} ● \frac{1}{3}$

8 $\quad \frac{3}{4} ● \frac{1}{2}$

9 $\quad \frac{1}{2} ● \frac{2}{4}$

10 $\quad \frac{9}{12} ● \frac{1}{2}$

11 $\quad \frac{3}{11} ● \frac{1}{2}$

12 $\quad \frac{7}{14} ● \frac{1}{2}$

13 $\quad \frac{5}{6} ● \frac{1}{2}$

14 $\quad \frac{7}{10} ● \frac{1}{2}$

15 $\quad \frac{1}{2} ● \frac{6}{14}$

16 $\quad \frac{4}{10} ● \frac{1}{2}$

17 $\quad \frac{1}{2} ● \frac{4}{5}$

18 $\quad \frac{4}{15} ● \frac{1}{2}$

19 $\quad \frac{5}{13} ● \frac{1}{2}$

20 $\quad \frac{1}{2} ● \frac{7}{9}$

21 $\quad \frac{1}{4} ● \frac{1}{2}$

Name _____

Relating Fractions to One Half (continued)

Compare. Write >, <, or = for each ●.

22 $\frac{1}{2}$ ● $\frac{1}{7}$

23 $\frac{1}{2}$ ● $\frac{5}{8}$

24 $\frac{2}{6}$ ● $\frac{1}{2}$

25 $\frac{4}{8}$ ● $\frac{1}{2}$

26 $\frac{7}{12}$ ● $\frac{1}{2}$

27 $\frac{5}{14}$ ● $\frac{1}{2}$

28 $\frac{1}{2}$ ● $\frac{1}{5}$

29 $\frac{13}{24}$ ● $\frac{1}{2}$

30 $\frac{1}{2}$ ● $\frac{9}{20}$

31 **Math Reasoning** Write 3 fractions with denominators of 16, 20, and 32 that are less than $\frac{1}{2}$.

32 Maggie has 7 dolls. Three of them have brown hair and 2 of them have black hair. Do the brown-haired dolls represent more or less than $\frac{1}{2}$ of Maggie's dolls?

_____

33 A jar contains 12 marbles. Seven are blue, 4 are red, and 1 is white. Do the blue marbles represent more or less than $\frac{1}{2}$ of the marbles?

_____

34 **Test Prep** Choose the correct letter for each answer.

Find the fraction that is more than $\frac{1}{2}$.

A $\frac{10}{24}$ **B** $\frac{10}{21}$ **C** $\frac{8}{16}$ **D** $\frac{8}{15}$

35 Find the fraction that is less than $\frac{1}{2}$.

F $\frac{4}{5}$ **G** $\frac{4}{8}$ **H** $\frac{3}{9}$ **J** $\frac{3}{4}$

© Scott Foresman

Name _____

1 Which symbol would complete the statement?

$$\frac{1}{2} \bullet \frac{7}{13}$$

A $>$ **C** $=$

B $<$ **D** $+$

2 Mom told Jason not to eat more than $\frac{1}{2}$ of the soup in the pot. Which of the following is the greatest amount of soup Jason can eat?

F $\frac{1}{4}$ of the soup

G $\frac{2}{4}$ of the soup

H $\frac{3}{4}$ of the soup

J $\frac{5}{6}$ of the soup

3 Which statement is false?

A $\frac{6}{12} = \frac{1}{2}$ **C** $\frac{1}{2} < \frac{10}{20}$

B $\frac{5}{11} < \frac{1}{2}$ **D** $\frac{1}{2} > \frac{3}{7}$

4 Missy bought 42 marbles. Twenty-four of the marbles were yellow. Which is true?

F Less than half are yellow.

G More than half are yellow.

H Half of the marbles are yellow.

J All of the marbles are yellow.

5 Which statement is true?

A $\frac{1}{2} = \frac{9}{18}$ **C** $\frac{5}{9} < \frac{1}{2}$

B $\frac{3}{7} > \frac{1}{2}$ **D** $\frac{10}{20} < \frac{1}{2}$

6 Which is not less than $\frac{1}{2}$?

F $\frac{3}{8}$ **H** $\frac{1}{4}$

G $\frac{4}{6}$ **J** $\frac{2}{5}$

7 Which symbol would complete the statement?

$$\frac{26}{52} \bullet \frac{1}{2}$$

A $>$ **C** $=$

B $<$ **D** $+$

8 Which is more than $\frac{1}{2}$?

F $\frac{4}{11}$ **H** $\frac{8}{13}$

G $\frac{5}{12}$ **J** $\frac{6}{15}$

Oral Directions Choose the correct letter for each answer.

© Scott Foresman

Three sheets of glass have thicknesses of $\frac{5}{16}$ inch, $\frac{3}{4}$ inch, and $\frac{5}{8}$ inch. Which sheet of glass is thickest?

Comparing and Ordering Fractions

Example

Compare: $\frac{4}{12} \bullet \frac{7}{9}$

Rewrite the fractions using the same denominator.
Think: What number has 7 and 9 as factors?

$$\frac{4}{12} = \frac{12}{36} \qquad \frac{7}{9} = \frac{28}{36}$$

Compare the new fractions: $\frac{12}{36} < \frac{28}{36}$

Write the comparison using the original fractions: $\frac{4}{12} < \frac{7}{9}$

Compare. Write >, <, or = for each ●.

1 $\frac{1}{4} \bullet \frac{3}{4}$

2 $\frac{5}{10} \bullet \frac{3}{10}$

3 $\frac{2}{3} \bullet \frac{5}{9}$

4 $\frac{7}{9} \bullet \frac{28}{36}$

5 $\frac{6}{15} \bullet \frac{2}{5}$

6 $\frac{10}{14} \bullet \frac{4}{7}$

7 $\frac{3}{5} \bullet \frac{7}{12}$

8 $\frac{4}{14} \bullet \frac{2}{5}$

9 $\frac{4}{7} \bullet \frac{2}{9}$

10 $\frac{1}{5} \bullet \frac{2}{8}$

11 $\frac{3}{8} \bullet \frac{2}{6}$

12 $\frac{4}{6} \bullet \frac{5}{9}$

Comparing and Ordering Fractions (continued)

Compare. Write >, <, or = for each ●.

13 $\dfrac{3}{5}$ ● $\dfrac{7}{15}$ **14** $\dfrac{8}{10}$ ● $\dfrac{13}{15}$ **15** $\dfrac{2}{8}$ ● $\dfrac{1}{4}$

16 $\dfrac{7}{10}$ ● $\dfrac{3}{4}$ **17** $\dfrac{6}{14}$ ● $\dfrac{3}{7}$ **18** $\dfrac{8}{12}$ ● $\dfrac{5}{6}$

Write each set of fractions in order from least to greatest.

19 $\dfrac{1}{4}, \dfrac{6}{7}, \dfrac{3}{5}$ **20** $\dfrac{5}{8}, \dfrac{8}{10}, \dfrac{2}{7}$ **21** $\dfrac{5}{9}, \dfrac{10}{12}, \dfrac{5}{7}$ **22** $\dfrac{3}{9}, \dfrac{12}{15}, \dfrac{5}{6}$

_____   _____   _____   _____

23 **Math Reasoning** Give 3 fractions with different denominators that are less than $\dfrac{2}{3}$.

_____

24 Jim's height is 4 feet, $3\dfrac{3}{4}$ inches. Rex's height is 4 feet, $3\dfrac{3}{8}$ inches. Joan's height is 4 feet, $3\dfrac{7}{16}$ inches. Who is the tallest? Who is the shortest?

_____

25 Two students are writing stories. Eric's story is $\dfrac{2}{3}$ of a page. Jason's story is $\dfrac{5}{8}$ of a page. Whose story is longer?

_____

26 **Test Prep** Choose the correct letter for the answer.

Which fraction is greater than $\dfrac{5}{9}$?

A $\dfrac{3}{6}$ **B** $\dfrac{1}{3}$ **C** $\dfrac{7}{18}$ **D** $\dfrac{2}{3}$

Name _____

1 Which list shows the fractions in order from least to greatest?

A $\frac{4}{4}, \frac{3}{4}, \frac{1}{3}$ C $\frac{3}{4}, \frac{4}{5}, \frac{1}{3}$

B $\frac{1}{3}, \frac{4}{5}, \frac{3}{4}$ D $\frac{1}{3}, \frac{3}{4}, \frac{4}{5}$

2 Andrew said he ate more than $\frac{1}{2}$ of his sandwich. Which of the following could Andrew not have eaten?

F $\frac{3}{9}$ H $\frac{5}{8}$

G $\frac{6}{10}$ J $\frac{2}{3}$

3 Which statement is NOT correct?

A $\frac{6}{9} = \frac{2}{3}$ C $\frac{3}{4} > \frac{8}{12}$

B $\frac{5}{6} < \frac{2}{5}$ D $\frac{2}{3} < \frac{13}{15}$

4 Which symbol would complete the statement

$$4\frac{7}{18} \bullet 4\frac{2}{3}?$$

F $>$ H $=$

G $<$ J $+$

5 Which statement is correct?

A $3\frac{2}{3} < 3\frac{10}{15}$ C $2\frac{7}{10} < 2\frac{3}{5}$

B $5\frac{1}{2} < 5\frac{6}{8}$ D $1\frac{3}{5} < 1\frac{6}{20}$

6 Mario correctly identified $\frac{2}{3}$ of the birds that the bird club saw on a walk. Betty identified $\frac{1}{2}$, Tami identified $\frac{3}{5}$, and Saul identified $\frac{11}{15}$. Which person correctly identified the most birds?

F Mario   H Tami

G Betty   J Saul

7 The diameters of a set of copper pipes are $\frac{3}{8}$ inch, $\frac{1}{4}$ inch, $\frac{7}{16}$ inch, and $\frac{5}{12}$ inch. Which shows the pipes in order from the least to the greatest diameter?

A $\frac{5}{12}$ in., $\frac{3}{8}$ in., $\frac{1}{4}$ in., $\frac{7}{16}$ in.

B $\frac{1}{4}$ in., $\frac{3}{8}$ in., $\frac{5}{12}$ in., $\frac{7}{16}$ in.

C $\frac{1}{4}$ in., $\frac{3}{8}$ in., $\frac{7}{16}$ in., $\frac{5}{12}$ in.

D $\frac{5}{12}$ in., $\frac{7}{16}$ in., $\frac{3}{8}$ in., $\frac{1}{4}$ in.

Oral Directions Choose the correct letter for each answer.

Alana hiked for 45 minutes and then rode a bike for twice as long. Write a mixed number to show how many hours she spent hiking and biking. Show the number on a number line.

Name _____

Example 1

Write $\frac{14}{3}$ as a mixed number.

Divide the numerator by the denominator.

$$3\overline{)14} \\ \underline{-12} \\ 2$$

with quotient 4 above.

Write the quotient as the whole number.
Write the remainder as the numerator of the fraction. $4\frac{2}{3}$
Use the same denominator.

Example 2

Write $2\frac{3}{4}$ as an improper fraction.

Multiply the denominator by the whole number ⟶ 2×4

and add the numerator. ⟶ $+ 3 = 11$

Write the result over the denominator. $\frac{11}{3}$

....

Change each improper fraction to a mixed number or a whole
number, and change each mixed number to an improper fraction.

1 $1\frac{2}{5}$ **2** $\frac{5}{3}$ **3** $\frac{7}{6}$ **4** $2\frac{1}{7}$

_____   _____   _____   _____

5 $\frac{9}{3}$ **6** $4\frac{4}{7}$ **7** $\frac{14}{5}$ **8** $5\frac{2}{9}$

_____   _____   _____   _____

Mixed Numbers (continued)

Change each improper fraction to a mixed number or a whole number, and change each mixed number to an improper fraction.

9 $3\frac{2}{7}$

_____

10 $\frac{7}{3}$

_____

11 $\frac{7}{2}$

_____

12 $1\frac{1}{10}$

_____

13 $\frac{9}{4}$

_____

14 $2\frac{2}{7}$

_____

15 $\frac{14}{2}$

_____

16 $6\frac{4}{9}$

_____

Write an improper fraction and a mixed number or whole number for each picture.

17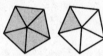

_____

18

_____

19

_____

20 **Math Reasoning** If an improper fraction has a numerator and denominator that are equal, then what will the equivalent whole number always be?

_____

21 There are 12 eggs in a carton. Mrs. Hudson has 15 eggs. Use a mixed number to describe how many cartons of eggs Mrs. Hudson has.

_____

22 **Test Prep** Choose the correct letter for the answer.

Change $\frac{15}{4}$ to a mixed number or whole number.

A $2\frac{7}{4}$　　**B** $3\frac{4}{3}$　　**C** 4　　**D** $3\frac{3}{4}$

Name _____

1 The distance from Springfield to Middleton measures $1\frac{3}{4}$ inches on the map. Which is the distance written as an improper fraction?

A $\frac{6}{4}$ **C** $\frac{9}{4}$

B $\frac{7}{4}$ **D** $\frac{13}{4}$

2 How is the improper fraction $\frac{20}{8}$ written as a mixed number?

F 2 **H** $3\frac{1}{2}$

G $2\frac{4}{8}$ **J** $3\frac{5}{8}$

3 Which fraction describes the shaded areas?

A $\frac{3}{8}$ **C** $\frac{19}{8}$

B $\frac{8}{19}$ **D** $\frac{24}{8}$

4 Which letter is at $2\frac{1}{4}$ on the number line?

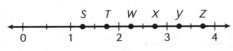

F T **H** V

G U **J** W

5 Which number does Point R represent?

A $\frac{3}{5}$ **C** $\frac{5}{3}$

B $\frac{2}{3}$ **D** 5

6 How is the improper fraction $\frac{23}{6}$ written as a mixed number?

F $4\frac{1}{6}$ **H** $3\frac{2}{3}$

G $3\frac{5}{6}$ **J** 3

7 Melissa's puppy weighs $8\frac{1}{8}$ pounds. Which is the weight written as an improper fraction?

A $\frac{1}{64}$ pound   **C** $\frac{64}{8}$ pounds

B $\frac{57}{8}$ pounds   **D** $\frac{65}{8}$ pounds

8 Which mixed number describes the shaded areas?

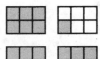

F $3\frac{1}{6}$ **H** $3\frac{1}{2}$

G $3\frac{1}{4}$ **J** $3\frac{5}{6}$

Oral Directions Choose the correct letter for each answer.

Use four different digits to make a fraction equal to 2.

Name _____

Fractions Greater than One

Example 1

Write $\frac{14}{3}$ as a mixed number.

Divide the numerator by the denominator.

Write the quotient as the whole number.

Write the remainder as the numerator of the fraction.

Use the same denominator.

$$\longrightarrow \quad 3\overline{)14}$$
$$\frac{-12}{2}$$
$$4\frac{2}{3}$$

Example 2

Write $2\frac{3}{4}$ as an improper fraction.

Multiply the denominator by the whole number and add the numerator.

2×4
$+\ 3 = 11$

Write the result over the denominator.

$\frac{11}{3}$

- -

Write each improper fraction as a mixed number, and write each mixed number as an improper fraction.

1 $2\frac{2}{5}$ **2** $\frac{7}{3}$ **3** $\frac{7}{4}$ **4** $1\frac{1}{7}$

_____   _____   _____   _____

5 $\frac{9}{2}$ **6** $4\frac{4}{10}$ **7** $\frac{16}{5}$ **8** $5\frac{2}{12}$

_____   _____   _____   _____

Name _____

Fractions Greater than One (continued)

Write each improper fraction as a mixed number, and write each mixed number as an improper fraction.

9 $2\frac{2}{7}$ _____

10 $\frac{13}{3}$ _____

11 $\frac{6}{4}$ _____

12 $1\frac{3}{10}$ _____

13 $\frac{11}{4}$ _____

14 $2\frac{2}{11}$ _____

15 $\frac{15}{2}$ _____

16 $6\frac{4}{15}$ _____

Compare. Write >, <, or = for each ●.

17 1 ● $\frac{5}{6}$

18 1 ● $\frac{5}{7}$

19 $\frac{9}{6}$ ● 1

20 $\frac{11}{9}$ ● 1

21 $\frac{7}{8}$ ● 1

22 $\frac{5}{5}$ ● 1

23 **Math Reasoning** Write 7 as a fraction with a denominator of 4. _____

24 The class is breaking into groups of 7. Use a mixed number to describe how many groups can be made if there are 24 students in class. _____

25 **Test Prep** Choose the correct letter for the answer.

Change $\frac{15}{4}$ to a mixed number.

A $2\frac{7}{4}$ **B** $3\frac{4}{3}$ **C** 4 **D** $3\frac{3}{4}$

Name _____

1 A play lasts for $2\frac{1}{4}$ hours. Which shows this number of hours as an improper fraction?

   A $\frac{5}{2}$ **C** $\frac{7}{4}$

   B $\frac{3}{4}$ **D** $\frac{9}{4}$

2 Mr. Benson cut sheets of red construction paper into sixths. Justine picked up 8 of the pieces. Which fraction shows how much paper Justine picked up in all?

   F $\frac{3}{4}$ sheet   **H** $1\frac{1}{3}$ sheets

   G $1\frac{1}{4}$ sheets   **J** 8 sheets

3 Which improper fraction is equal to 1?

   A $\frac{9}{8}$ **C** $\frac{5}{1}$

   B $\frac{3}{2}$ **D** $\frac{2}{2}$

4 What is the improper fraction $\frac{17}{3}$ written as a mixed number?

   F $4\frac{5}{3}$ **H** $5\frac{3}{4}$

   G $5\frac{2}{3}$ **J** $6\frac{1}{3}$

5 A talent show has 11 acts. Each act is 10 minutes long. How long does the talent show last not including intermission?

   A $1\frac{1}{10}$ hours   **C** $2\frac{3}{4}$ hours

   B $1\frac{5}{6}$ hours   **D** $6\frac{1}{5}$ hours

6 What is the mixed number $3\frac{1}{6}$ written as an improper fraction?

   F $\frac{9}{6}$ **H** $\frac{21}{6}$

   G $\frac{19}{6}$ **J** $\frac{24}{6}$

7 Which statement is true?

   A $\frac{4}{5} > 1$

   B $\frac{8}{8} > 11$

   C $\frac{10}{9} > 1$

   D $\frac{9}{10} > 1$

8 Which number belongs in the ▣ to make the statement true?

$$\frac{▣}{7} > 1$$

   F 5   **H** 7

   G 6   **J** 8

Oral Directions Choose the correct letter for each answer.

© Scott Foresman

Tools Contents

Fraction Strips

1

$\frac{1}{2}$	

$\frac{1}{3}$		

$\frac{1}{4}$			

$\frac{1}{5}$				

$\frac{1}{6}$					

$\frac{1}{8}$							

$\frac{1}{10}$									

$\frac{1}{12}$											

10 × 10 Chart

Name _____

Base-Ten Blocks, Set 1

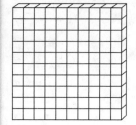 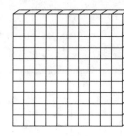 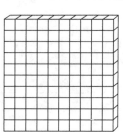

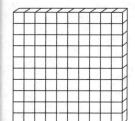 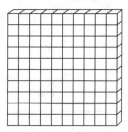

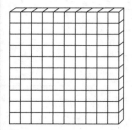 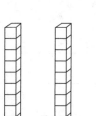 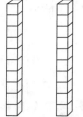

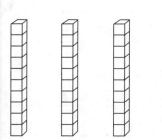 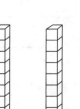 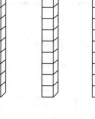  

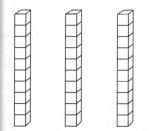

Fraction Strips

1

$\frac{1}{2}$	

$\frac{1}{3}$		

$\frac{1}{4}$			

$\frac{1}{5}$				

$\frac{1}{6}$					

$\frac{1}{8}$							

$\frac{1}{10}$									

$\frac{1}{12}$											